FUN FACT FILE: SPACE!

20 FUN FACTS ABOUT ASTEROIDS AND COMETS

By Arielle Chiger and Adrienne Houk Maley

Gareth Stevens
PUBLISHING

Please visit our website, www.garethstevens.com. For a free color catalog of all our high-quality books, call toll free 1-800-542-2595 or fax 1-877-542-2596.

Library of Congress Cataloging-in-Publication Data

Chiger, Arielle.
20 fun facts about asteroids and comets / by Arielle Chiger and Adrienne Houk Maley.
  p. cm. — (Fun fact file: space!)
Includes index.
ISBN 978-1-4824-0792-1 (pbk.)
ISBN 978-1-4824-0994-9 (6-pack)
ISBN 978-1-4824-0791-4 (library binding)
1. Asteroids — Juvenile literature. 2. Comets — Juvenile literature. 3. Solar system — Juvenile literature.
I. Chiger, Arielle. II. Title.
QB651.C45 2015
523.44—d23

First Edition

Published in 2015 by
Gareth Stevens Publishing
111 East 14th Street, Suite 349
New York, NY 10003

Copyright © 2015 Gareth Stevens Publishing

Designer: Sarah Liddell
Editor: Greg Roza

Photo credits: Cover, p. 1 wongwean/Shutterstock.com; p. 5 Mopic/Shutterstock.com; p. 6 Cook Chris/Photo Researchers/Getty Images; p. 7 Artur Kamalov/iStock/Thinkstock.com; p. 8 PaulFleet/iStock/Thinkstock.com; p. 9 Stocktrek Images/Getty Images; p. 10 NASA/Handout/Getty Images News/Getty Images; p. 11 Andrea Danti/Shutterstock.com; p. 12 Andre Viegas/Shutterstock.com; p. 13 Mopic/Shutterstock.com; p. 14 Neo Edmund/Shutterstock.com; p. 15 Elenarts/Shutterstock.com; p. 16 Space Frontiers/Stringer/Archive Photos/Getty Images; p. 17 Martin Gardeazabal/Shutterstock.com; p. 18 MARK GARLICK/Science Photo Library/Getty Images; p. 19 LobStoR/Wikimedia Commons; p. 20 Time Life Pictures/Contributor/Time & Life Pictures/Getty Images; p. 21 (Edmond Halley) Georgios Kollidas/Shutterstock.com; p. 21 (main) Digital Vision/Photodisc/Thinkstock.com; p. 22 (asteroids) Dabarti CGI/Shutterstock.com; pp. 22–23 (main) Giovanni Benintende/Shutterstock.com; p. 23 (comet) MarcelClemens/Shutterstock.com; p. 24 Digital Vision/Digital Vision/Getty Images; p. 25 Huntster/Wikimedia Commons; p. 26 Universal History Archive/Contributor/ Universal Images Group/Getty Images; p. 27 Mike Agliolo/Photo Researchers/Getty Images; p. 29 Vadim Sadovski/Shutterstock.com.

Printed in the United States of America

CPSIA compliance information: Batch #CS15GS: For further information contact Gareth Stevens, New York, New York at 1-800-542-2595.

Contents

Words in the glossary appear in **bold** type the first time they are used in the text.

Where Did You Come From?

Asteroids and comets have existed since our **solar system** formed about 4.5 billion years ago. A lot of rock and gas got scattered about while the sun, planets, and moons formed. There was probably enough **material** to make another Earth. Much of this material was pushed away from the sun far out into the solar system.

Comets and asteroids were made from this swirling, rocky, dusty, icy material. Thanks to **gravity**, these space objects **orbit** the sun, just like the planets do.

The sun's gravity is so great that it has kept all the planets, asteroids, and comets in a continuous orbit for billions of years.

FACT 1

Comets are sometimes called "dirty snowballs" or "snowy dirtballs."

Comets are made up of ice, dust, rocks, and small amounts of other materials. The surface of a comet is dark and uneven. Comets are often covered with rough craters, perhaps from being hit by other comets and asteroids for millions of years.

Comets have three main parts. The rocky, icy core is called the nucleus. The cloud around the nucleus is called the coma. Many comets also have a tail of gas and dust.

tail

coma

nucleus

Asteroids have uneven surfaces. They don't have enough gravity to become round like planets and moons.

FACT 2

Asteroids are rockier and drier than comets.

Asteroids are mostly rock and metal with small amounts of other materials. Asteroids contained a lot of water when they formed. But the solar system was very hot then, and most of the water turned to gas. However, some asteroids still contain a lot of water.

Many asteroids are very small—sometimes as tiny as a grain of sand.

FACT 3

There are FAR more asteroids near Earth than comets.

So far, **astronomers** have **identified** nearly 5,000 comets in the solar system. That may seem like a lot, but scientists have identified more than 600,000 asteroids in the solar system! Astronomers think there are about 200 asteroids that are larger than 60 miles (97 km) in **diameter**.

Asteroid Adventure

Asteroids live close to home.

Asteroids are ancient remnants, or leftover material, from the beginning of our solar system. Asteroids formed closer to the sun than comets. The inner planets and Earth's moon have craters from being hit by asteroids when they were forming.

This photograph of craters on Mercury's surface was taken by an unmanned spacecraft in 2008.

Asteroids love company.

Asteroids tend to group together. The rocky planets formed when many asteroids came together. Today, the main **region** where asteroids can be found is called the asteroid belt. This belt, or long trail of asteroids, orbits the sun between the orbits of Mars and Jupiter.

About half the mass of the asteroid belt is contained in the four largest asteroids— Ceres, Vesta, Pallas, and Hygeia.

Vesta

The asteroids in the asteroid belt never joined together to make a planet. Scientists believe this is because Jupiter's gravity causes them to crash together instead of grouping together.

FACT 6

If all the asteroids in the asteroid belt were smashed together, they still wouldn't be as large as the moon.

Asteroids range from small grains of dust to giant rocks hundreds of miles in diameter. The largest known asteroid is called Ceres. Ceres is about 590 miles (950 km) wide. All the asteroids in the asteroid belt combined have less mass than the moon.

FACT 7

A shooting star is really a burning asteroid.

Sometimes small asteroids called meteoroids enter Earth's **atmosphere**. This causes them to heat up and even burst into flames! This is what's happening when you see a shooting star. Meteoroids that burn up in Earth's atmosphere are called meteors. Comets may also leave behind pieces that form shooting stars.

Sometimes meteors are big enough to crash into Earth's surface. Then, these rocks are called meteorites.

A large asteroid impact with Earth would cause widespread destruction. However, this only happens about once every 100,000 years.

FACT 8

Large asteroids have hit Earth in the past and may again in the future.

On February 15, 2012, an asteroid named 2012 DA14 flew close to Earth. Researchers were able to study this asteroid up close. The closest it got to the planet was about 17,150 miles (27,600 km) above Earth's surface.

13

FACT 9

NASA (National Aeronautics and Space Administration) searches for and tracks asteroids to protect our planet from them and to learn about them.

The NASA Near Earth Objects (NEO) Program keeps track of, or monitors, asteroids and comets that pass close to Earth. The information they find helps us understand the origin of our solar system. One of their most important tasks is to search for and identify asteroids that could hit Earth.

In 1801, Giuseppe Piazzi, a Sicilian monk, discovered Ceres while looking through a telescope. Ceres is so large that Piazzi thought it was a planet at first.

Ceres

Vesta

FACT 10

We're soon going to know more about asteroids.

Astronomers want to know more about asteroids. The Hubble Space **Telescope** has captured images of Ceres, and astronomers have many questions about it. In 2007, NASA sent a space **probe** toward the asteroid belt. It will reach Ceres in 2015 and then move on to study Vesta.

FACT 11

Most comets are larger than cities.

Comets come in many sizes, but even the smallest are pretty big. A comet's nucleus can be anywhere from 0.6 mile to 62 miles (1 to 100 km) in diameter. A comet's coma can grow as large as the planet Jupiter!

Comet 17P/Holmes is only about 2.2 miles (3.5 km) wide. However, in 2007, its coma suddenly grew to a size larger than the sun.

Comets sometimes have tails.

Comets formed farther away from the sun than asteroids. Ice, dust, and rock were trapped together as comets formed. As a comet's orbit brings it closer to the sun, the ice inside the comet melts. This frees gas and dust, which form a "tail."

Solar winds push the dust and gas from a comet. That means the tail always points away from the sun. Tails can stretch for millions of miles behind a comet.

17

You need more than your fingers and toes to count comets!

Comets form in two regions far away from the sun. The Kuiper (KY-puhr) Belt could have a trillion, or a thousand billion, comets. The Oort Cloud is much larger and much farther away. Astronomers think the Oort Cloud could contain 2 trillion comets!

asteroid belt

Kuiper Belt

Oort Cloud

Objects located in the Oort Cloud and Kuiper Belt are called Trans-Neptunian Objects. That means they're farther away from the sun than the planet Neptune.

The holes in Tempel's nucleus may be from ice that melted long ago. This suggests that ice acted just like glue to hold the dust and rock together.

The center of a comet is like a sponge.

In 2005, NASA's Deep Impact spacecraft placed a heavy probe in the path of comet Tempel 1. When they crashed together (shown above), scientists discovered that much of Tempel's nucleus is filled with holes, somewhat like a sponge. The surface is much softer than scientists thought it would be.

FACT 15

Comet Shoemaker-Levy 9 looked like a string of pearls.

In 1992, Jupiter's gravity broke passing comet Shoemaker-Levy 9 into 21 pieces. These pieces orbited Jupiter until 1994, when they crashed into the planet. Many people on Earth used telescopes to watch this happen. The 21 comet pieces burst into flames just before crashing.

The Hubble Space Telescope captured these images of Shoemaker-Levy 9, and it became known as the "string of pearls" comet.

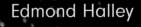
Edmond Halley

Halley's comet is called a short-period comet. This means it takes under 200 years to make a full orbit around the sun. Long-period comets have orbits that can last many thousands of years.

FACT 16

Mark your calendars—Halley's comet will be back.

Halley's comet is perhaps the most well-known comet. Once every 76 years, it passes close enough to Earth for us to see it without a telescope. The last time Halley's comet was visible from Earth was 1986. It will make another visit around 2061.

Compare and Contrast

Asteroids and comets are very different, but they also have some things in common. The information here will help you remember how they are the same and how they are different.

ASTEROIDS

- chunks of rock and metal
- more than 600,000 identified asteroids in solar system
- range from dust size up to 600 miles (1,000 km) across
- more than 150 large asteroids have one or more moons
- most are found in the asteroid belt

COMETS

- chunks of ice, rock, and dust
- grow tails as they approach the sun
- more than 5,000 identified in solar system
- trillions more in the Kuiper Belt and Oort Cloud
- nucleus is sponge-like

BOTH

- remnants of giant clouds of rock and gas from the formation of the solar system
- the sun's gravity keeps them in orbit
- they change their course of direction due to gravitational "tugs" from different planets
- when they break apart, smaller pieces appear as shooting stars when they enter Earth's atmosphere

FACT 17

The gravity of planets can affect where comets and asteroids go.

Comets have a very long, elliptical—or oval-shaped—orbit. Asteroids often follow a more circular orbit. However, the gravity of planets in the solar system, particularly Jupiter and Saturn, can pull on comets and asteroids, causing their orbits to change.

The irregular shapes and sizes of asteroids and comets cause them to wobble as they orbit the sun.

Comet Lovejoy, a Kreutz sungrazer, was discovered in 2011.

sun

comet Lovejoy

FACT 18

Comets and asteroids vaporize as they dive through the solar atmosphere.

Sungrazers are comets and asteroids that pass very close to the sun. Some pass so close the sun's atmosphere causes them to **vaporize**! In the late 1800s, German astronomer Heinrich Kreutz found that many sungrazers are pieces of a comet that broke up over 800 years ago.

FACT 19

Astronomers think comets and asteroids were like water delivery trucks for a young Earth.

Since comets are mostly water and ice, it's believed that early comet crashes into Earth's surface may have delivered water to the young planet. Asteroids contain some water, too, so they may have contributed water deliveries as well.

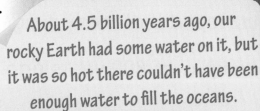

About 4.5 billion years ago, our rocky Earth had some water on it, but it was so hot there couldn't have been enough water to fill the oceans.

Many people think the dinosaurs died off when a comet or asteroid struck Earth 65 million years ago. This allowed other creatures to survive.

FACT 20

Asteroids and comets may have helped shape life on Earth.

Many scientists believe that long ago, when asteroids and comets frequently hit Earth, they caused great changes to the planet's **environment**. Many creatures died. Those that survived needed to **adapt** in order to live in this newly changed environment.

Space Rocks!

Asteroids and comets are fascinating balls of space material. They're pushed around by planetary gravity, and they're the reason we sometimes see shooting stars. These space bodies have been around for billions of years, and most will be around for billions more.

Do you think that comets and asteroids had an impact on how Earth and the creatures living on it came to be? Astronomers will continue to study them until they find the answers.

Some astronomers wonder if comets and asteroids helped life flourish on planets outside our solar system.

Glossary

adapt: to change to suit conditions

astronomer: a person who studies stars, planets, and other heavenly bodies

atmosphere: the mixture of gases that surround a planet or star

diameter: the distance from one side of a round object to the other through its center

environment: the natural world in which a plant or animal lives

gravity: the force that pulls objects toward the center of a planet or star

identify: to find out the name or features of something

material: the matter that makes up an object

orbit: to travel in a circle or oval around something, or the path used to make that trip

probe: an unmanned spaceship

region: a large area that has features that make it different from other nearby areas

solar system: the sun and all the space objects that orbit it, including the planets and their moons

telescope: a tool that makes faraway objects look bigger and closer

vaporize: to turn to vapor, or gas. Also, to completely destroy.

For More Information

Books

Block, Dakota. *Exploring the Solar System*. New York, NY: PowerKids Press, 2013.

Mist, Rosalind. *Could an Asteroid Hit the Earth? Asteroids, Comets, Meteors, and More*. Chicago, IL: Heinemann Library, 2006.

Woolf, Alex. *An Asteroid Strike*. Chicago, IL: Capstone Heinemann Library, 2014.

Websites

Asteroids and Comets
science.nationalgeographic.com/science/space/solar-system/asteroids-comets-article/
Explore both asteroids and comets with the help of some amazing photos.

Asteroids, Comets, and Meteorites
www.jpl.nasa.gov/asteroidwatch/asteroids-comets.cfm
Find out what NASA considers to be a potentially hazardous object in space.

Comets and Meteors
www.esa.int/esaKIDSen/SEM059WJD1E_OurUniverse_0.html
Read more about comets, meteors, and asteroids on the European Space Agency's website.

Index